Economical
Recipes

ISBN: 978-1913725099

This edition published 2025 by Nigel Gourlay, Ashworth House, Long Lane, Chapel-en-le-Frith, High Peak, SK23 0TF.
email: ngourlay@gmail.com

Reproduced from archival material kindly supplied by Kath Sizeland, originally owned by Mrs G. Leach.

FOREWORD

In 1918, the ladies of Chapel-en-le-Frith, a market town in England's picturesque High Peak, collected this book of 'economical' recipes which were printed locally and sold for ninepence in aid of orphans.

Today, the recipes stand as a fascinating insight into the struggles of ordinary families in a typical northern town, after four years of war and hardship. Many of the family names are still common in Chapel, now belonging to the great-grandchildren of the book's contributors.

Hearty thanks to all who
have so kindly
contributed
Recipes.

FISH, MEAT, AND SAVOURIES.

~~~~~

Savoury Fuffs.

½ lb potatoes	2 ozs flour
Yolk of 1 egg	Pepper
Cold meat	Salt

Mash potatoes lightly (they must be dry and floury), add yolk of egg, flour and seasoning, blend well into a dry dough, roll out, cut into small pieces, and in each put a small quantity of meat minced, or rissole mixture, fold over, moisten edges, press firmly together, and fry golden brown, serve hot.

<div align="right">MRS. N. C. GOODWIN.</div>

Mock Hare.

1 lb fillet of beef or steak

A little butter or beef dripping

Cut the beef into slices about the size of a joint of hare, and fry them in the fat. Have ready in a stewpan a gravy made as follows :—1 pint of stock or water, 5 or 6 cloves, a small quantity of sliced onion, pepper, salt, and gravy browning. Place the fried pieces of beef in this gravy and stew gently for 1½ or 2 hours. Thicken and serve with red currant jelly.

<div align="right">MRS. N. C. GOODWIN.</div>

Ramakins.

Two eggs	2 ozs of grated cheese
1 teasp. of flour	2 tablesp. of cream
2 ozs of melted butter	

Well beat the eggs, and add to the other ingredients, and bake in small tins a ¼ of an hour.

MRS. DRURY,

Surprise Balls

Take a breakfastcupful of rice, wash it thoroughly, place it in a saucepan with a breakfastcupful of boiling water, and let it gently simmer till the rice has absorbed all the water. Then add quickly a breakfastcupful of scalded milk with salt to taste, and cook until the rice is quite soft. Let the rice get cold and then mix in carefully a tablespoonful of grated cheese, form the rice into balls the size of ordinary potatoes, and fry quickly in hot fat, drain the balls and serve very hot with tomato sauce or plain. These surprise balls are very delicious.

G. M.

Cheese Pudding.

4 ozs cheese	Pinch of carbonate
1 teacupful milk	of soda
1 dessertspoonful flour	Pepper
1 egg	Salt

Put the milk into a pan, and grate cheese into it. Mix, flour, pepper, salt and soda into a smooth paste and add to milk, Bring all to gentle boil and when smooth pour into pudding dish, add the egg well beaten. Place in oven till brown and risen, serve hot.

MRS. W. HALL.

Savoury Pudding.

Stale bread soaked in milk or water, 1 shredded onion, suet or dripping, sage. parsley, pepper and salt, 1 egg   Flour, just enough to make it hold together, pour in a greased tin, and bake.

MISS EVANS.

Lentil Roast.

½ lb lentils	A little sage
2 onions	1 pint of stock (either
2 ozs butter	vegetable or the
6 ozs bread crumbs	other.)

Wash the lentils and soak over night in cold water, cook with the onions and stock until tender, add bread crumbs, also butter and seasoning of herbs, Grease a cake tin, dust it over with brown bread crumbs, put in the mixture and bake a nice brown. Turn out, and serve with a good gravy and either apple sauce or red currant jelly.

MRS. CRAVEN.

Turban of Lentils and Rice.
A MEATLESS DISH.

¼ lb red lentils   Half a teacup stock

5

¼ lb rice	1 dessertsp. bread-
1 onion	crumbs.
⅓ oz fat	1 teasp. chopped
Small teasp. mixed	parsley
herbs.	Salt and pepper

Wash the lentils and just cover them with tepid water and simmer for 1 hour. Boil the rice and drain it. Chop onion finely and fry until browned. Then mix all ingredients together with the exception of the crumbs. Grease a cake tin and powder it with fine crumbs, fill it with the mixture and bake in a moderate oven for 1 hour. Turn the 'turban' out and serve with potatoes and a green vegetable. Sufficient for 3 persons.

ANON.

Meat and Vegetable Pudding with Potato.

Pudding.

¾ lb meat	2 teasp. flour
4 ozs haricot beans	½ teasp. salt
1 lb potatoes	¼ teasp. pepper
2 to 3 small onions	Water

Suet Pastry.

½ lb flour	6 ozs suet
¾ teasp. baking powder	Cold water to
¼ teasp. salt	mix

Pudding. Cut the meat into thin slices, mix the seasonings and flour on a plate and dip the pieces

6

of meat into the seasoned flour, cook the haricot beans and cut up the other vegetables, line a greased bowl with the suet pastry, put in half the meat and the vegetables, add the water, and fill up with the rest of the meat. Place on pastry and press the edges together, cover with a scalded and floured pudding cloth, put the pudding into a saucepan of boiling water and cook steadily for 2½ hours.

MRS. ATTENBOROUGH.

Beef Olives.

3 tablesp. bread crumbs	½ oz chopped bacon
1 tablesp. chopped parsley	½ teasp. salt
A few sprigs of marjoran & thyme	1 egg
	¼ teasp. pepper

Place the bread crumbs, parsley, thyme, bacon, salt etc. in a basin and bind together with beaten egg.

Cut 1 lb of beef steak into thin slices about 6 inches long and 2 inches wide. Flour both sides and place a small ball of forcemeat on these pieces of beef. Roll up and tie. Put 1 oz of butter in stewpan, when boiling add olives and brown over, cover with water or stock and simmer 1 hour. Add pepper, salt and flour to gravy.

MISS TITMAS.

Savoury Omelette.

2 eggs   Salt
1 oz butter   1 oz chopped ham
Pepper   Chopped parsley

Boil the ham ten minutes, then mince finely. Separate the eggs, beating the whites quite stiff. Beat the yolks, add the ham, seasoning, parsley, mix very lightly with the whites. Grease well the omelette pan. Melt 1 oz of butter in it. Pour in the mixture. Stir very lightly till it begins to set. Shake constantly to keep from sticking.

MISS TITMAS.

Cheese and Macaroni.

Boil 6 ozs of macaroni, broken into 1 inch lengths, in salted water till tender. Strain and place in deep dish with 1 oz of butter or margarine and 2 ozs of grated cheese, seasoning to taste, including a few grains of cayenne, add 3 tablesp. of water in which the macaroni was boiled, and shake over the top 2 ozs more of grated cheese. Bake $\frac{1}{4}$ of an hour in moderate oven or until the top is nicely browned, and serve very hot in the same dish.

MISS TAYLOR, The Mount.

Toad in the Hole.

$\frac{1}{2}$ lb sausages   1 egg
4 ozs flour   1 saltsp. salt
1 gill milk   A dust of pepper

Into a well-greased pie dish, pour the following

8

batter over the sausages Beat up the egg, and add the milk, make a smooth batter by pouring the milk and egg gradually into the flour, salt, and pepper. This is better mixed an hour or two before wanted. A little baking powder may be added at the last. Bake 1 hour in a moderate oven.

MRS. NEEDHAM, Lower Eaves.

Meat Pudding.

½ lb of cooked meat (minced or chopped), ½ lb of mashed potatoes, 1 cooked onion (chopped), 1 beaten egg (or 1 teacup of milk). 1 breakfastcup of brown bread crumbs, 1 teasp. mixed herbs, salt to taste, ¼ lb of cooked-split peas (or haricot beans if preferred), add bread crumbs, potatoes, herbs, salt and peas (or beans) to meat, mix with egg or milk, strain 1 hour in greased basin Cook with greased paper.

MISS HEYWOOD, Manchester.

Tasty Meat Dish.

6 ozs medium oatmeal	1 teasp. of parsley
2 ozs chopped suet	1 teasp. of herbs
2 ozs ,, meat (cooked)	Seasoning
2 onions, cooked and chopped	A little gravy or vegetable stock to mix in

Then mix all ingredients with sufficient stock to form a soft mixture that drops easily from a spoon. Put in a well-greased basin, cover with a pudding cloth and boil steadily for 3 hours. Turn out, serve with gravy,

MRS. LOWE.

Savoury Mutton.

Into a deep pie dish put a layer of sliced potatoes, a layer of sliced tomatoes, and a layer of sliced onions, add pepper and salt to taste, then a layer slices of cold mutton, then again potatoes, tomatoes, and onion, fill up the dish with gravy or stock, and bake two hours in a moderate oven, cold beef may be used instead of mutton.

MRS. NEEDHAM, Lower Eaves.

Hot Haricot Cutlets.

1 pint of beans	Piece of margarine
1 teasp. carbonate soda	the size of a walnut
A little sage	1 small onion

Soak beans over night in water with the soda, next morning strain off the water and put beans in pan with margarine, sage, chopped onion and water to cover. Boil till quite soft, then put through the mincer. Turn on to the board and shape into rounds. Flour these a little and fry in smoking fat till brown. A little mashed potato can be added to the beans and a few chopped nuts.

MRS. W. BRIDGE.

Kidneys Stewed in Gravy.

4 kidneys   1 large onion
1 ozs flour   Pepper
1 pint water   Salt

Mix the flour with the water to a paste with salt
and pepper to taste. Skin and core the kidneys,
and cut into eight or ten pieces. Then put them in
the paste with the onion which must be finely
chopped. Put all in a pan and allow to simmer
for an hour, stirring occasionally.

MISS TITMAS.

Mock Lobster Cutlets.

2 tablesp. ground rice   Pepper
1 chopped onion   Anchovy sauce
Salt   Teacupful milk

Boil until a stiff paste, stirring all the time
Crumble bread crumbs on dish, pour over them the
mixture, let it set, and when set, cut up and fry
until golden brown. Serve with anchovy sauce.

MRS CRAVEN.

Sardine Eggs.

4 hard boiled eggs   8 sardines
Pepper and salt   1 dessertsp. butter

Cut the eggs in half while still warm, take out
the yolks. Place in a basin and beat up yolks with

12

cleaned sardines, oiled butter, pepper and salt. Garnish with parsley and serve with toast.

MISS FARTHING.

Stuffed Marrow.

Peel the marrow and cut it down the centre, core it and stuff it with forcemeat, either onion or fowl forcemeat, fill it in, bind it round with a piece of tape put a greased paper round it and bake it in the oven (till tender) about $\frac{3}{4}$ of an hour, serve with gravy or sauce.

MISS C. PINK.

Salmon Mould.

Small tin salmon	1 egg
1 slice breadcrumbs	1 teasp. essence of
Potatoes, 1 lb when	anchovies
boiled	Pepper & salt to taste

Boil the potatoes, beat them up well with the salmon and bread crumbs. Beat the egg, then add with the other ingredients. Put in a mould and cover with greased paper, steam 1 hour. Can be eaten cold with mayonnaise sauce, or cut into slices when cold and fried and used with parsley sauce.

MISS M. RIGHTON, The Greggs.

Green Pea Cutlets.

$\frac{1}{4}$ lb dried split green	$\frac{1}{4}$ pt milk or stock
peas	Seasoning

Pinch of mixed herbs	Egg
$\frac{1}{2}$ oz butter	Bread crumbs
$\frac{1}{4}$ oz flour	

Soak and cook the peas. Make a sauce of the fat, flour and milk. Put in the peas, add seasoning and herbs and sufficient bread crumbs to make a firm mixture. Make up into any shape preferred, coat with egg or milk and bread crumbs and fry in hot fat, serve with brown gravy or mint sauce.

MRS. FODEN.

Salmon Mould.

A large tin of salmon, turn into a mixing bowl and remove all bones and dark coloured skin, break up salmon with a wooden spoon, add a teaspoon of chopped parsley, break in two fresh eggs (or cook's eggs). Crumble a thick slice of bread, pepper and salt, mix all well together, put into a greased mould or basin and cover with a greased paper and steam for one hour.

MRS. R. HYDE.

Egg Pie.

Boil hard 2 or 3 eggs, cut in thick slices and lay them in a pie dish. Make some sauce, either anchovy or cheese sauce, and pour over the eggs. Cover over with mashed potatoes, put a few little pieces of margarine on the top, and cook till brown.

MISS ANDERSON.

Beef Roly Poly.

½ lb shoulder steak   3 onions
3 ozs suet   Pepper to taste
½ lb flour   Salt to taste

Put meat through mincing machine, chop onions. Make suet paste, put in meat and onions, roll, boil in cloth 2 to 3 hours and bake in moderate oven. Sufficient for 5 or 6 persons.

MRS. PRESTON.

Vegetable Curry.

1 large apple   ⅛ teasp. ground ginger
2 onions   2 ozs butter or margarine
Vegetables (any)   2 teasp. curry powder
½ cucumber   1 small teasp. salt
½ lb rice   ½ pint milk
1 tablesp cocoanut   Flour
  (dessicated)

Peel the apple and cucumber, and slice onions and apple thinly. Cut cucumber into pieces, melt the butter in the saucepan, dust vegetables with flour. Now place onions and apple in the butter and cook for 20 minutes with lid on saucepan ; then add the cucumber, and cook another 15 minutes. Add grated cocoanut, curry powder, ground ginger, salt and milk. Mix vegetables, add them to the curry and simmer ½ hour. Dish up with border of rice round the vegetables.   MRS. WARMAN.

Egg and Potato Pie

Shell 3 to 5 hard-boiled eggs and cut them in

slices Mash some potatoes with butter and milk, season with salt and white pepper and a little nutmeg. Line the bottom of an earthenware dish with the potato, and then a layer of egg sliced. Sprinkle some chopped parsley over, and cover with some white sauce. Continue alternate layers of potato, egg, sauce and parsley. Cover the top with mashed potatoes, and put small pieces of butter on top, or brush with white of egg, and bake $\frac{1}{2}$ an hour.

MRS. WARMAN.

Boston Baked Beans.

1 quart haricot beans, cover with cold water, and soak overnight, In morning drain cover with fresh water, heat slowly keeping water below boiling point, and cook until the skins burst, which is best determined by taking a few beans on the tip of a spoon and blowing on them, when skins will burst if sufficiently cooked. Drain beans, scald rind of $\frac{3}{4}$ lb fat salted pork (or unsalted), cut through the rind every $\frac{1}{2}$ inch, making cuts an inch deep. Put beans in jar and bury pork in, leaving rind exposed. Mix 1 tablesp. salt, 1 tablesp. treacle, and 3 tablesp. sugar, add cup of boiling water, and pour over beans, then add enough more boiling water to cover beans. Cover stew jar, put in oven and bake slowly 6 to 8 hours, uncovering the last hour of cooking that rind may become brown and crisp. Add water as needed.

MRS. BANCROFT.

PUDDINGS.

~~~

Cheap Spongecake Pudding.

3 penny sponge cakes
Peel and juice of half a lemon
1 egg
A small piece of butter (or margarine)
A very little sugar and milk

Soak the cakes in a little milk, and mix them with the juice and grated peel of half a lemon, a piece of butter, a very little sugar and 1 egg. Beat all together, and bake in a quick oven.

MRS. DRURY.

Apple and Sago Pudding.

½ pint milk	Sugar, or substitute
½ pint water	to sweeten
½ pint stewed apples	1 dried egg
and juice	A little powdered spice
3 ozs small sago	(if liked) or lemon
	rind if preferred.

Put the milk and water on to boil, when boiling sprinkle in the sago, stir and work till quite clear and very thick. Mix in the stewed apple and juice, add sweetening and spice if used. Cool for 5 minutes, then beat in the egg prepared according to directions. Turn the mixture into a greased basin, cover with greased

17

paper, and steam for 1 hour. Turn out carefully
on to a hot dish, and pour over it a little warmed
apple jelly as sauce, or a sauce made from water
in which the rinds and cores of the apples have
been boiled, colour with a little cochineal,
thicken with cornflour and slightly sweeten.
(Semolina may be used instead of sago).

MRS. MILLER.

War-time Pudding.

8 ozs mashed potatoes	2 tablesp. treacle
2 ozs ground rice	2 teasp. baking
1 egg	powder
1½ oz fat	

Steam 1½ hours.

MRS. PONTEFRACT.

Colchester Pudding.

3 ozs butter, ¼ lb sugar. Whisk until they
become the consistency of cream, then add by
degrees 5 ozs of flour, 2 eggs whisked to a stiff
froth, 1 teasp. baking powder.

Boil 2½ hours, and serve with custard. Line
the basin with jam.

MRS. FRITH.

Barley Pudding.

Barley	1 egg
2 tablesp. brown sugar	1 gill milk
2 ozs. currants	

18

When making barley water for invalids, do not throw the barley away; after it is strained off, make into a pudding with above ingredients.

Half fill a pie dish with the barley—add the sugar and currants. Beat egg and milk, and pour over barley, &c., and stir all together. Sprinkle over a little finely-chopped suet and grated nutmeg, and bake 1 hour in a hot oven. This is a very wholesome pudding for children.

MRS. COLLETT.

War-time Pastry.

6 ozs flour	4 ozs suet or lard
5 ozs rice-flour	1 teasp. baking powder
5 ozs fine oatmeal	Salt

Put flour and meal into a basin with baking-powder and salt. Put fat, with about equal bulk of water into a small pan, and bring nearly to boil. Then stir it into the ingredients in basin, and mix thoroughly with a knife. Shape into dumpling or roly-poly, tie in a cloth and boil, serve hot with syrup, or syrup and ginger may be mixed in before cooking.

If baking pastry is required, use 6 ozs of fat. Roll out at once, or the crust breaks up before it can be lifted to the dish.

MRS. TALLENT-BATEMAN.

Dripping Pudding.

½ lb flour   Teasp. baking powder
1½ ozs dripping   Pinch of salt

Rub dripping into flour, add baking powder and
salt, mix with a little milk and water. Steam for
1½ hours, when turned out ready for serving pour
a little syrup or jam over the top.

MISS ANDERSON.

Heaton Pudding

Cut the crust off thin rounds of bread and butter,
spread lemon curd between each 2 rounds, and fill
a well greased pudding dish, then mix a custard of
1 egg. 1 gill of milk and sugar, pour over the bread
etc. in dish, cover with flat dish and leave for 1 hour,
then cook in moderate oven till a nice brown, turn
out, and serve very hot.

MRS. SEDDON.

Sago Plum Pudding.

3 tablesp. sago   1 oz margarine
⅕ breakfastcup flour   2 tablesp. sugar
⅕ breakfastcup ground   ½ teasp. carbonate
   rice   soda
1 cup raisins

Soak sago overnight in milk or water, mix all
ingredients well, put in greased basin and steam for
3 hours.

MRS. PARTINGTON.

Treacle Sponge.

¼ lb fine oatmeal   ¼ lb mashed potatoes
3 ozs suet   1 teasp. baking powder
1 teasp. ground ginger   Treacle

Mix with treacle and milk, put in greased basin and steam for 2 hours.

MISS D. PARTINGTON.

Ginger Sponge Pudding.

Mix well, 1 teasp. baking powder with ½ lb flour, then rub in 4 ozs lard, add 1 teasp. of ground ginger and 2 ozs of sugar. Mix well, then add 1 tablesp. of golden syrup, 1 egg and ½ gill of milk, beat thoroughly together, then pour into a well greased basin and steam 2 hours.

MISS SMITH.

Treacle Pudding.

½ lb flour
1 teasp. baking powder   ½ lb treacle
3 ozs finely chopped suet   1 teasp. sugar

Warm the treacle and mix it with other ingredients, beat to a batter, and pour the mixture into a well greased basin or mould, tie over with greased paper and either boil or steam for 3 hours.

MISS SMITH.

CAKES.

Chocolate Fingers.

Cream 2 ozs of butter with $1\frac{1}{2}$ ozs of sugar, beat in 1 egg, add $1\frac{1}{2}$ ozs of flour and a $\frac{1}{4}$ teasp. baking powder. Bake in very small flat tin lined with buttered paper. When cold, ice made as follows :— boil 1 oz of grated chocolate with 2 teasp. of water, take off, add 2 ozs of iceing sugar, spread on cake and cut into small fingers.

M. L.

Shortbread.

8 ozs flour	A few drops of
5 ozs margarine	flavouring or
2 ozs sugar	chopped almonds

Beat margarine and sugar to a cream, stir and knead in flour, turn out on a board, beat with rolling pin, make into a round, pinch edges, and bake in slow oven till brown.

MRS. SCHUNCK.

Gingerbread.

1 lb flour	1 teasp. carbonate of
1 lb fine oatmeal	soda dissolved in a
$\frac{1}{2}$ lb lard or dripping	little milk
$\frac{1}{2}$ lb sugar	1 lb golden syrup
1 oz ground ginger	A little lemon peel

Mix soft and bake in a moderate oven 1¾ hours.

MRS BANCROFT, Duffield.

Ginger Cake.

1 lb flour	1 teacupful milk
¼ lb lard	1 dessertsp of car-
3 ozs brown sugar	bonate of soda
¾ lb syrup	1 large teasp. ground
	ginger

Warm syrup and milk to dissolve soda in, rub the lard into the flour, add sugar and ginger, pour in gradually and mix well with the other ingredients, pour into a well-greased baking tin, and bake about an hour in a moderately hot oven.

MRS. BARNES

Oatmeal Biscuits.

½ lb. oatmeal	1 dessertsp. sugar.
¼ lb. flour	1 teasp. baking powder
2 ozs. butter	Pinch of salt

MRS. STURM.

Quaker Oats Biscuits.

½ lb dough	1 teasp. sugar
½ lb Quaker Oats	1 teasp. baking powder
3 ozs butter or lard	

Knead all together.

MRS. STURM.

Scones

1 lb flour	$\frac{1}{4}$ oz. cream of tartar
6 ozs butter	1 oz sugar
$\frac{1}{4}$ oz carbonate of soda	1 cupful warm milk

Mix all ingredients together, roll out, cut in shapes, and bake on a buttered tin.

MRS W JACKSON.

Shrewsbury Biscuits.

8 ozs flour	1 teasp. baking
4 ozs butter or margarine	powder
4 ozs sugar	1 egg

Cream butter and sugar together, add egg, then beat in the flour by degrees, turn out on to a floured board, knead lightly, cut into rounds and bake on a greased tin. A few caraway seeds may be added if liked.

MRS. W, JACKSON,

Oatmeal Scones.

3 ozs sugar	$\frac{1}{2}$ teasp. baking powder
8 ozs medium oatmeal	Teacupful milk
6 ozs flour	$\frac{1}{2}$ teasp. carbonate soda
4 ozs lard or dripping	A little salt

Dissolve carbonate of soda in warm milk, add to rest of ingredients to a very stiff paste, roll out and cut to desired shape.

MRS. MAYLE.

25

26

Small Buns.

$\frac{1}{2}$ lb flour	2 eggs
$\frac{1}{4}$ lb margarine	Currants or flavouring
$\frac{1}{4}$ lb sugar	

Cream butter and sugar together, add flour and eggs (well beaten) by degrees, and a small teasp. of baking powder last of all, bake in quick oven about 15 minutes.

E. STEEPLES.

American Apple Cake.

Cream together 1 cup sugar, $\frac{1}{2}$ cup butter, $\frac{1}{2}$ teasp. salt, $\frac{1}{2}$ teasp. ground cloves, 1 teasp. cinnamon, 1 cup raisins, 1 teasp. carbonate of soda dissolved in a little hot water, stir in 1 cup stewed sour apples. Let all foam together over the ingredients in the bowl, beat well together and add gradually $1\frac{3}{4}$ cups flour, bake in moderate oven about 55 minutes.

MRS. STABLES.

Rice Rock Cakes.

3 ozs rice flour	$1\frac{1}{2}$ ozs flour
3 ozs cornflour	Pinch of salt

Rub into these, 4 ozs lard or margarine and 4 ozs sugar, mix with well beaten egg and a little milk, drop on baking tin, leave 2 in between each, bake in a quick oven 15 to 20 minutes.

MRS. STABLES.

Drop Scones.

¾ breakfastcup flour   Dessertsp. sugar
Small piece of butter or   Dessertsp baking
   margarine   powder
1 egg

Mix to light batter and fry in tablespoonfuls on
hot tin well greased with lard. Turn over when set
and brown, can be buttered and eaten while hot or
allowed to cool and rolled up with a little butter
and raspberry jam.

MRS. W. HALL.

Sandwich Cake.

2 ozs flour   1 egg
2 ozs rice flour   1 teasp. (small
1 oz each margarine &   baking powder
  lard, or all margarine   1½ ozs sugar

Cream fats and sugar, add flour (mixed with rice
flour) and egg (well beaten) alternately, beat well,
add baking powder and put in greased sandwich
tin, bake about 20 minutes in a moderate oven.

L. H.

Quaker Oat Shortbread.

½ lb quaker oats   2 tablesp. flour
¼ lb dripping or lard   1 teasp. baking powder
2 ozs sugar   Milk
1 tablesp. syrup   Salt

Beat dripping and sugar to a cream, add syrup

and dry ingredients and mix to a stiff paste with a little milk, bake in very slow oven 2 hours.

MRS. E. WALKER.

Oatmeal Buns.

½ lb fine oatmeal	A pinch of spice
3 ozs margarine	A pinch of salt
½ desertsp. golden syrup	3 ozs stoned dates
1 gill milk	1 teasp. carbonate
2½ ozs flour	of soda

Mix together all the dry ingredients, rub in the fat, dissolve the syrup in the milk and mix into a dough, divide into 12 buns and bake 20 minutes.

MRS. ATTENBOROUGH.

Date Cake without Eggs.

½ lb flour	¼ lb brown sugar
¼ lb lard	½ oz candied peel
¼ lb cut up dates	¼ teasp. all spice
3 ozs raisins	¼ wineglass of vinegar

Mix 1 teasp. of soda in half a gill of milk, mix together and bake in a moderate oven for 1 or 1½ hours (add the vinegar last).

MISS BRAMWELL, Isca.

Potato Cakes.

Rub ¼ lb lard with 1 lb of cold boiled potatoes, add a pinch of salt and half a teasp. of baking powder and a little flour. Stir in a small quantity of warm milk, roll out and bake in a moderate oven until a light brown.

D. J.

Ginger Sponge Cake.

10 ozs flour	$\frac{1}{2}$ oz ground ginger
3 ozs butter(margarine)	2 tablesp. golden
3 ozs sugar	syrup
1 oz peel	$\frac{1}{2}$ teasp. carbonate
1 egg	of soda

Beat butter and sugar to a cream, add flour etc., dissolve the soda in 2 tablesp of milk, and add the beaten egg, beat thoroughly, pour into tin lined with greased paper, bake in a moderate oven about 40 minutes.

ANON.

Fruit Cake.

12 ozs flour	1 teasp. mixed spice
$\frac{1}{2}$ lb sugar	2 ozs walnuts
$\frac{1}{4}$ lb butter	$\frac{1}{4}$ lb fruit and if
1 teasp. baking powder	stone fruit $\frac{1}{2}$ lb
1 teasp. carbonate of soda	Milk to make moist

MISS DUGDALE, Lytham.

Thick Gingerbread.

1$\frac{1}{4}$ lbs flour	$\frac{1}{4}$ lb butter
1 lb treacle (warmed)	$\frac{1}{2}$ oz ground ginger
$\frac{1}{4}$ lb brown sugar	1 oz candied peel
1 good teasp. of carbonate of soda dissolved in a	

little lukewarm milk, rub the butter into the flour, add the sugar, ginger and candied peel. Then add the treacle, and last of all the carbonate of soda mixed with enough lukewarm milk to make the mixture into a rather stiff paste, bake in a Yorkshire pudding tin, lined with buttered paper, and, if liked, when partly baked put slices of candied peel or blanched almonds on the top, and glaze with milk and sugar as for tea cakes.

MRS. DALTON, Burrfields.

Parkin.

1 lb oatmeal	1 lb syrup or treacle,
$\frac{1}{4}$ lb lard or margarine	or half of each
Salt	

Melt syrup and fat together, and stir salted oatmeal in slowly with knife. bake very slowly.

MRS. TALLENT BATEMAN.

Steamed Cake.

2 cupfuls flour	2 ozs fat
2 tablesp. syrup or treacle	1 tablesp. sugar
	$1\frac{1}{2}$ tablesp. cocoa
$\frac{1}{2}$ teasp. carbonate of soda	Teacup of sour milk

Mix dry ingredient, rub in fat, pour in treacle and milk to make a stiff batter. Pour into tin, and put in steamer for 1 hour. place in oven for 10 minutes to harden.

MRS. PARKER, Oak House.

Oatmeal Biscuits.

1 cupful of oatmeal	½ cupful sugar
1 cupful flour	2 ozs lard or butter

Mix the meal and flour, and rub in the lard, then add the sugar and a pinch of salt. Dissolve ½ a teasp. of carbonate of soda in a little hot water and sufficient cold milk to mix into a stiff dough, roll out on board and cut into shapes and bake in a moderate oven

MRS. STAMPER.

War Cake.

1 lb flour	2 ozs walnuts
½ lb margarine	2 teasp. baking powder
3 or 4 ozs sugar	1 teasp. carbonate of
½ lb dates	soda

in a gill of warm milk with one tablesp of vinegar.

Mix and bake in slow oven 1½ hours.

MISS FARTHING.

Ginger Buns.

6 ozs flour	½ oz ground ginger
¼ lb golden syrup	1 oz peel
2 ozs butter or margarine	1 egg
	¼ teasp. carbonate soda
2 ozs sugar	A little milk

Melt the margarine, syrup and sugar, beat all well together, adding soda the last. Put in small tins and bake in moderate oven about 20 minutes. This quantity makes about 1 doz buns.

MRS. MILLER.

Plain Ginger Cake.

½ lb flour
4 ozs of sugar
2 teasp. ground ginger (more according to taste)
1 teasp. of pudding spice
½ teasp. carbonate of soda
A little salt
2 ozs. lard
1 breakfastcup of sour milk

Mix dry ingredients together, rub in the lard, and mix with the milk.

MRS. LYALL.

Soda Cake.

1 lb flour
½ lb sugar
6 oz butter
1 teasp. baking powder
2 teasp. egg powder
1 teasp. carbonate soda
1 teasp cream of tartar
Pinch of salt
A few currants if liked

Rub butter into dry ingredients and mix with milk. Bake slowly.

MISS BENNETT.

Oatmeal Biscuits

2 teacupfuls flour	1½ teasp. ginger
1 teacupful oatmeal	1 teasp. carbonate soda
½ teacupful ground rice	mixed in a little milk
	4 ozs sugar

About 2 tablesp. of treacle in a little milk and mix into a stiff paste.

Roll out and cut into rounds, bake from 13 to 15 minutes.   MISS N. DAW.

War Cake.

1 cup sultanas	1 scant cup lard or
1 cup water	margarine

Boil for 5 minutes, when cold add :—

1 cup sugar	1 teasp. carbonate
2 cups flour	of soda
1 teasp baking powder	1 teasp spice

Mix well, bake in a cool oven about 2 hours.

War Cake.

12 ozs flour	½ teasp. spice
6 ozs margarine	1 teasp. carbonate
6 ozs sugar	of soda
8 ozs currants	¼ spoonful ginger
2 ozs peel	½ pint milk

Mix soda with flour, rub in fat, add all ingredients and mix well, line a cake tin with 2 folds of newspaper and 1 of well greased white, allowing the paper to come well above the tin.   Bake in moderate oven 2 hours, this cake improves with keeping, will be quite moist in 2 months' time.

Miss F. Richer,

Ladies and Gents' Outfitter,

"BON MARCHE,"

CHAPEL-EN-LE-FRITH.

Millinery, Baby Linen, and Fancy Goods.

JOHN SIDEBOTHAM,

MARKET STREET,

CHAPEL-EN-LE-FRITH,

For all kinds of

Gold and Silver Jewellery, Plate.

Old Furniture, China and Silver
bought and sold.

Tel. 31.

Ed. Carrington,

Ironmonger,

CHAPEL-EN-LE-FRITH.

Lamps, Incandescent Goods, China, Earthenware, etc. Oils for Lubricating and Burning.

36

Ginger Cake.

6 ozs flour	1 small teasp carbonate
3 ozs oatmeal	of soda
1 teasp, egg powder	3 ozs lard or dripping
1 small teasp. ginger	melted with
	3 dessertsp, syrup

Mix with a litte warm milk, if not sweet enough, 1 oz sugar may be added, bake in a moderate oven.

MRS. COLLIER.

Madeira Cake.

$\frac{3}{4}$ lb flour	4 eggs
7 ozs butter	1 teasp. baking
8 ozs castor sugar	powder

The grated rind off 2 lemons. Slice of citron peel.

Beat the butter and sugar to a cream, whisk the eggs until frothy, then stir them gradually into the butter, mix the flour with the lemon and baking powder. Mix the dry ingredients in lightly with the eggs, and bake 1 hour in a greased tin.

MRS. GIDDINGS.

Almond Cakes.

$\frac{1}{4}$ lb butter	1 tablesp. cream
$\frac{1}{4}$ lb sugar	1 tablesp. brandy
$\frac{1}{4}$ lb flour	or sherry
2 ozs ground almonds	$\frac{1}{2}$ teasp. of baking
2 eggs	powder

MRS. BAYNE.

Shortbread.

1 lb flour $\frac{1}{2}$ lb castor sugar   10 ozs butter

Rub to a stiff paste.   MRS. BAYNE.

PRESERVES.

Marrow Cream.

4 lb marrow	Juice of 3 lemons
4 lb sugar	and rind of 2
4 ozs butter	

Steam marrow till soft, beat to a cream, add sugar etc., and cook till quite soft.   MRS. SCHUNCK.

Lemon Cheese.

12 ozs sugar	2 tablesp. of Cook's
4 ozs margarine	eggs(soaked over night)
2 small lemons	1 tablesp. ground rice

Take the grated rind and juice of lemons, put in a stew pan with the eggs, butter, sugar and ground rice, stir over the fire until it is about the consistency of honey.   MRS. GREENHOUGH.

Apricot Jam.

Soak 1 lb dried apricots in 3 pts. of cold water for 12 hours, then boil all up till tender, (about $\frac{1}{2}$ au hour). Blanch and shred 1 oz almonds, add to the apricots with $2\frac{1}{2}$ lbs granulated or lump sugar, and boil till it sets. This will make about 7 lbs of jam.   MRS. SEDDON

Green Tomato Pickle.

Slice 10 lbs full grown green tomatoes into dish and sprinkle well each layer with salt. Let them remain all night. next day strain and put the tomatoes into a

38

preserving pan with 2 quarts of vinegar, 2 lbs moist
sugar, 1 lb sliced onion, $\frac{1}{4}$ oz each of cinnamon, cloves
and whole peppercorns, $\frac{1}{2}$ teasp. cayenne. Boil all
gently until quite tender, then bottle and cork well.
Ready for use at once. MISS M. WHITEHEAD.

Tomato Jam.

1 lb tomatoes, $\frac{3}{4}$ lb sugar, the juice of 1 lemon
and the grated rind or a little ginger if preferred.
Put the tomatoes through a sieve, add the other
ingredients to the pulp and boil quickly for $\frac{1}{2}$ hour.
MISS ASPELL.

Crab Apple Jelly.

Wipe the fruit with a damp cloth and place in a
mug, adding sufficient water to immerse the fruit,
but the topmost layer should not be entirely covered
Place in a hot oven till the fruit is quite soft, then
let it drip through a jelly bag, add white sugar in
proportion of 1 lb to each pint of syrup, then boil
until it thickens sufficiently (do not boil more than
$\frac{1}{2}$ an hour and not less than 20 minutes.
MISS DAWE.

Marrow Cream.

2 lbs marrow
2 lbs sugar
$\frac{1}{4}$ lb butter

The rind and juice
of 3 lemons

Steam the marrow until it is tender, strain and
mash or put through a sieve, mix all ingredients to-

39

gether and after all are dissolved, boil for 20 minutes. This will be found very good in tart or sponge sandwiches, it is not known from lemon curd and is much cheaper.　　　　　　　　　MISS ASPELL.

Marrow Lemon Cheese.

4 lb marrow cut small, steam till tender, and mash very fine, put into pan and add 3 lbs sugar, ½ lb butter, grated rind and juice of 4 lemons, simmer until it becomes a smooth paste.

MRS. PARKER, Oak House.

MISCELLANEOUS.

Vegetable Hot Pot.
(For 4 people).

1 teacup haricot beans	2 medium-sized onions
½ teacup pearl barley	12 crushed peppercorns
4 or 5 medium sized potatoes	3 bay leaves
2 carrots	Add parsley, thyme, and celery

40

2 parsnips Salt to taste
1 swede turnip (small)

Cut the vegetables into small pieces. Put the ingredients into a fairly large saucepan, fill half full of cold water, bring to the boil, and simmer for about 2 hours. MRS F. BENNETT.

Home-made Chocolate.

$\frac{1}{4}$ lb. cocoa butter 1 dessertsp. corn
$\frac{1}{2}$ lb. Epp's sweetened flour
  Bivouac Chocolate 1 teasp. vanilla
  Powder flavouring

Melt cocoa butter well, and add to it the other ingredients Stir well, pour into a flat dish and let stand till well set. MRS. COLLETT.

Polish for Brass and Copper.

Dissolve 2 ozs oxalic acid in one quart of water, and add $\frac{1}{4}$ to $\frac{1}{2}$ lb. of rotten stone. Apply with plenty of elbow-grease. T.P.

Pan Polish.

1d. powdered bath brick 2 pkts. Hudson's
1d. whitening Dry Soap
  Mix all together MISS J. DAWE.

Mayonnaise.

2 yolks of eggs	1 gill salad oil
3 teasp. vinegar	Pepper
½ teasp made mustard	Salt

Put yolks, salt, pepper, mustard and vinegar in a basin. Mix and add oil drop by drop.

MRS. BRITTON.

Imitation Whipped Cream.

½ oz gelatine	1½ ozs sugar
¼ pt cream	¾ pt milk Flavouring

Soak gelatine in milk for 15 minutes, then dissolve gently over fire, strain into bowl, and when nearly cold, beat well and add the cream which must be previously whisked.

MRS. W. BRIDGE.

Emulsion.

½ pt cod liver oil	1 small tin Nestle's
¼ pt lime water	milk
1 oz glycerine	1 teasp. oil of almonds

Put in bottle and shake up well.

MRS. J. G. WALKER.

Potato Starch.

Wash and peel 2 or 3 potatoes, grate them into a clean pan and cover with cold water, leave them for 2 or 3 hours, then strain the water into another pan and let it stand for another 2 hours. When the water is drained off, there will be a sediment at the bottom. On this pour sufficient boiling water to make it thick, and there is your starch. M.A.WILSHAW